with love, from me x

AF408730

shermya modupe

BookLeaf Publishing

India | USA | UK

presentation by *bookleaf publishing*

web: www.bookleafpub.com

e-mail: info@bookleafpub.com

ISBN: 9789357611886

first edition 2022

dedication

this book is dedicated to you, my love. you know who you are and you know what you mean to me. thank you for being the muse that let my poetry grow wiser and deeper than ever before. i never knew what it really felt like to be in love with a poem until i fell in love with you. thank you.

acknowledgement

thank you to everyone who has supported me and inspired me this far. i know i can be difficult but i wouldn't be here, doing this, without you. to everyone i love and have loved, thank you. you have shaped me. you have made me realise what is good in this world and what is not. even those who i no longer share love with, these words are because of you too. thank you, endlessly, to you all.

preface

i have no intention of keeping you from my metaphors for long, i truly hope you enjoy them. i am no professional in this field, each of these poems are just an outpour of my immense emotions in that specific second. every poem is from a new experience and a new explosion of formidable love, whether bad or good, in my on and off relationship. i never thought i would be a poet, then never thought i would continue to write poetry, then never thought i would share my poetry in this way. poetry has a way of surprising you like that. it has encompassed my soul and i can't imagine a day without a metaphor whizzing past me. poetry feels like a tight hug and i hope that hug extends through ink and pages to reach you too. i wrote these poems when i was an entirely different version of myself but each and every one of these poems is the most genuine portrayal of first love i could give you. even though we are nothing like this anymore, these words were curated from the best and worst days of true love and i truly wish for you all to experience the joy in seeing your lover smile. there is nothing quite like it.

**- welcome to the writers, wannabes
and yet to be's**

more often than not, the poem has already been
written
a thousand times
in a thousand of the same and different ways
but it's a poet's job to fall in love and write
poetry on top of poetry to make more beautiful
poetry
and that is what makes your poetry so special
never forget that

- you saved me more

why do i fall for the ones who never like me
back
literally never
i really should stop doing that
it would save me a lot of time
it would save me a lot of sleep
it would save me a lot of missed assignments
it would save me a lot of tfl journeys
it would save me a lot of liver failures
it would save me a lot of pregnancy scares
it would save me a lot of secrecy
it would save me a lot of heartbreak hidden in
metaphors
it would save me a lot of walks
alongside moonlit pavements
a lot of pain, tears, sadness
it would save me
a lot
but then again
i wouldn't have met you

- a third time isn't always lucky

3

i deleted pictures of you today
then removed them from my 'my eyes only'
then unsaved them from all our chats
who knew something as efficient as social media
could make a break up three times as long

- i would die alone if it meant you were happy

you were the last person keeping me sane
without you, now, i feel like a crazy person
clinging to falling marbles
my brain feels like a sieve allowing my
happiness to slip through the cracks whilst
depression is growing in the corners of my mind
clouding my judgement, my future and my smile

you were the last person keeping me safe
you were the double lock on the door after
stepping past the welcome home mat
you were the one to calm my mind enough for
me to fall back into sheltered sleep
but now i feel as though safety was made for
everyone but me
as though your absence has forced me back into
the lonely dangers of life
you clearly weren't made for me but maybe
endless loneliness and perilous risk was
a lifetime commitment of intimacy to intense
abandonment

you were the last person keeping me happy
and you still you do

you just don't keep us happy anymore, because
there is no more us
the smile we once shared will split at the lips of
what once held our love
one half of a giggle will trail behind you
basking your footsteps in golden sunlight
whilst i sit in mournful patience waiting for
yours to find mine again

if your mother ever asked me i would say
i would fight if i could
but he has told me repeatedly to stop fighting
i would fight until my very last breath gives out
but i can see that every fight leaves him with a
scar
every battle leaves him with an open infected
wound
every punch leaves him with bruises in the shape
of the bouquet of flowers i am trying to give
and so,
every good soldier must learn when to put down
her weapons
admit defeat
and wave the white flag in surrender to the love
we both know he deserves
we know his heart is too precious for me to tear
it anymore

- maybe the ring will fit your finger better?

to his next lover
i am drunk right now
on the verge tears which will most definitely fall
by the end of this poem
i haven't let him go yet, you should know
but i wouldn't be surprised if our end was nigh
so i thought i would give you a helping hand
point a finger in the right direction
help your palms meet somewhere in the middle
even if it means i end up with no ring
at least some good would have come out of this
whole thing

to his next lover…

he will never eat a proper meal
he will complain about the price of an innocent
smoothie then buy 3 every time he shops but
also… he will never shop in bulk
he thinks thermal socks are the height of fashion
he has the strictest skin care routine but the
messiest bathroom
he hates small talk and loves a bit of tension
let him know how you feel at all times, he likes
to know

make him playlists
he gets cold easily
but will always refuse to admit it even if every
fibre of his being is shivering
so bring an extra sweater whenever you go out
wrap him up
cocoon him in all you have to offer
then put his hands in yours for extra measure

he loves a good cuddle
even when he tries to act all macho
hug him anyway
twirl your fingers through his curls as you lay in
bed
the sheets will swaddle you as you profess to
them the weight of your love in the stroke of a
cheek
he gives amazing hugs
i fell in love with how my nose fit perfectly
against his neck

meet his friends
they are so lovely
they're absolute idiots but they're hilarious
once they like you, life will be okay
even if you lose your own
and you are left stranded by structures you
thought would always support you
you know they're there in the background

they will mock you to the end of the earth and
back
but there is a small heart, hidden in a delicate
paper towel, beating and rooting for you behind
every joke

don't let him invest all his money in bitcoin...
for your own sake
you'll never hear the end of it when it inevitably
ends in decline

to his next lover...

never forget to admire his eyebrows
they are his pride and joy
and they're gorgeous, so it's a win win
tell him everyday that he is the reason brown
eyes are superior
even when he is adamant that blue eyes hold up
the sky and green ground the world in nature
tell him that his eyes are the reason you feel safe
enough to breathe again
the reason you are able to laugh
the reason you believe the world turns on its axis

he is so sensitive
i found this out the hard way
i hurt him
i fractured a little piece of his heart

and i lost the ability to breathe when i did so
don't do it again
treat him with the purest of intentions
he may never admit how he feels
but i promise you he feels it
so make him feel so loved
he is like a teddy bear in the freshest of snows
he is the only one worthy of your nose upon his
he deserves more than even he knows

take him on long car rides
i know he was really excited for me to pass my
test
drive up to university to see him
that's something i still long to do
drive through the deepest of valleys to his heart
and pitch up a tent
wait for a rare sighting
for him to open up his heart
for this romantic eclipse to occur
it will go down in history books
to be chosen by him is a phenomenon
it is unique
it is unthinkable
it is extraordinary

read to him before he goes to bed
let him drift off to sleep listening to luxurious
lines of poetry

allow him the privilege to fall in love with your
voice
he may never take interest in the actual storyline
but play him vocal melodies as the sunsets over
your romance novel

to his next lover…

his mum became one of my parents too
became the woman i wanted to show my first
tattoo
she became a reason why i wanted to see him
she made everything feel okay
my mum is amazing, make no mistake
but so is his
so cherish her
i may never get to again
that woman is a sunflower in a field of happiness
but don't forget to engage in tabletop
conversations with his dad too
you will leave their house ten times wiser every
single time
i hope they are impressed by what you bring to
the table
i hope they look at you and see future
granchildren
and i truly hope you are everything they want for
their son

make sure he has the conversation
the one still hiding in my reminders app
the one i tried to expel from his mind
tell him it's time for the conversation if he still
wants to have it
remind him it's never too late
and if the answer is still no
remind him he is not to blame
it is not his fault

pay for things for him
he'll try to stop you or try to pay you back but
treat him anyway
he is the one man i have always deemed worthy
of my money
unless it is for... bitcoin

take pictures of him
without him knowing, with him knowing, all the
time
he's camera shy until given the chance to flex
his jawline
he has the kind of face, the kind of energy, the
kind of persona, you will want captured
to remember for the rest of your life
so you never forget what it feels like to breathe
the same oxygen as him
to see the same sky as him
to live in the same minute as him

to blink your eyes knowing that within at least 1
second he may or may not blink his eyes too
the thought of that alone will make you okay
i promise

to his next lover…

he is a lightweight
let me say it again, just so you know what you're
in for
he is a lightweight
he hates wine but will drink it regardless if you
like it
just to enter into crimson stained evenings by
your side
he will try to make you drink the most
disgusting pints just to laugh at your reaction
he refuses to admit that magnums don't taste
nice
but then again i am the same
i guess we are both stubborn
and he will spend endless time calculating the
alcohol percentage to price ratio when buying
any drink
but i assure you
you will come to love his mathematical mind
it amazed me every single time and still does
but maybe that's simply because i still use my
fingers to count sometimes

maybe you will be a little smarter than i am
about it all
you won't fall silent in the face of long division
you won't crumble at the sight of a quadratic
equation
you won't be dumb enough to lose him
he is destined for greatness
when you meet him you'll be able to see a future
of stars in his eyes
he is the smartest person i know

bite his nose
it used to really annoy him
and maybe this is selfish of me because i hope if
you do this he will think of me
but do it anyway
do this one thing for me
because he knows if you do that you love him
and he deserves someone who loves him enough
to nibble on his nose

get a cat
get a fat cat named phil
that's what we talked about
he's a cat person, don't change that about him
it's what makes him so special
he made me a cat person
get a fat cat named phil
get an apartment

get kids you two will enjoy mocking for
character building purposes to nurture kids as
funny as he is
get a life filled with joy and drive and passion
get him everything he wants

to his next lover…

treat him with kindness
love him with everything you own
learn even more about him than i have
and make sure he smiles
for the rest of his life
make sure he smiles

with love, from me x

- does my appetite change after nineteen?

i once heard a quote that said:
"we as teenage girls will accept love in the form
of crumbs and still call ourselves full"
why is that?
you have given me nothing but crumbs and i
would call myself full for the rest of our lives

notice how i said "our"
our lives
intertwined between the full course meal i give
and the crumbs i get back
but i guess it's about quality not quantity, right?
if i convince myself enough that i can live off of
crumbs forever then maybe it'll be true
if i just squeeze my appetite between the palm of
my hands then maybe i won't desire anymore
than crumbs
i never thought you would be the one to seat me
across from my eating disorder again
not when you were the one who saved me

gluttony is not an attractive quality anyway

but there are only so many crumbs i can keep
picking off the floor before you stop dropping
them
before i crumble into a state of starvation
a depressive heap of malnutrition in dire need
of... crumbs
a rejected mound of hungry limbs never to be
fed again
i can feel you keeping your crumbs close to your
heart
you're not dropping them anymore
maybe you got peckish
i guess everyone gets bored of the girl who will
take crumbs in exchange for all the love she
could possibly give

somehow, hunger is not an attractive quality
either
i can't win

some would say it's a good thing
maybe it will allow me to find someone who can
actually cook
replenish my body
pick my mental state up off the floor and seat me
in front of a michelin star cook up
a bottomless brunch of love and affection
but right now
in this present moment

where i spend my nights in constant fear that
i might forget the way in which your lips taste
i am really hungry

and a crumb would do nicely

- lara jean would be proud

to all the pecks that never happened
to all the stolen kisses we could've had
to all the nose rubs we never felt dripping in
golden sunlight

i'm sorry we missed you
i'm sorry our paths never crossed
i think the correct term for that is star crossed
lovers
destined to be together but just not right now
now's not the right moment
our love's star hasn't reached its peak yet
it's not resting on top of the universe
and when i look into your eyes i know that's the
only place where we belong

so,
to all the pecks that never happened
sit tight
wait patiently
i am waiting along with you
i know he's taking his time
but i promise you that when i feel his hand slip
in between my fingers
or when he hugs for a little extra while longer

or when he looks in my eyes and knows
everything i am trying to hide
i know the wait will be worth it

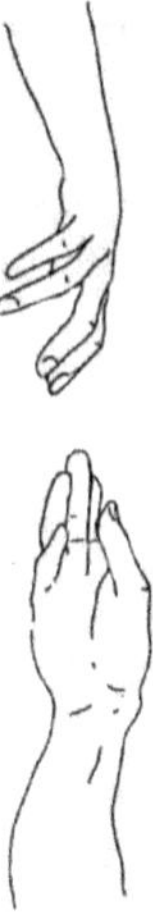

- addiction

i would do anything to have my heart broken by
you again and again for the rest of my life
because at least that would feel better than this
i took for granted our rocky relationship
the constant shipwrecks and on and off moments
because now our ship has capsized and i know it
will never be smooth sailing again

- emma stone was a great cruella

in defence of cruella de vil
has the world ever been blessed with someone as
beautiful as you?
i know of no one who could take animal print
and actually make it look good
no one who could walk into a room and turn
animal heads as well
but isn't that part of the joke
part of the appeal
part of the reason why people will never
understand the prowess of a woman like you
because they're asking the wrong question
so let me rephrase it

has the world ever been blessed with someone as
passionate as you?
someone who revels in all the things we are told
we are not supposed to be?
i know of no one who could spend an entire 3
hours, 23 minutes and 17 seconds chasing down
dogs; their dreams
god made the word devotion and you were the
first thing that came to mind
i may not be good at maths but i am 101% sure
that you are the epitome of poise
i could learn a thing or two from you

about passion
about the undying assurance that your love for
animal prints can carry you through an endless
franchise

i have only felt such passion around you, my
love
such infinite desire
to make up conversation just to hear your voice
i don't even know what a natural science is but
coming out of your mouth it is the closest thing i
imagine the sound of angels to be
soft
happy
beautiful
perfect

i would sell my soul to the devil to buy cruella's
car just to race you to the top of my heart
and if i won you'd have to let me fall in love
with you
because i'd happily let you break my heart into
101 white and black spots just to prove that
loving is something i can do
i trust you more than anyone i know
and maybe this time i'll take a tip from ms. de
vil and i won't leave

but how do you put forever in a tiny box?

get down on one knee
and give it away as if the weight of forever
means nothing
you see i'm not scared of the height or the
falling; that's just part of the thrill
i'm scared of what will happen when my body
hits the floor
and i know this is weird but there are times i
wish that God would turn you into animal fur so
i can feel you on my skin forever and never have
to spend another day without you

that's why sometimes when we hold hands i hold
a little too tight
and i don't let go
i'm sorry
i'm just chasing the same electric feeling cruella
gets from chasing dogs all day
forgive me
please
i just didn't know one squeeze of a hand could
give such joy
in defence of cruella de vil
i now understand the need to chase what makes
your heart race

but even cruella knows when the race must end
when to hang her coat up and to stop chasing
dogs that don't want to be caught

when such a beautiful metaphor is no longer
yours to wield
but if now is the time when i must put down my
fur coat
let me fold it the same way i would fold a
memory
carefully
ensuring none of the smiles would have the
chance to slip out of any of the pockets
softly
knowing that what i hold within my hands are
some of the happiest moments of my life
slowly
making sure the coat is as perfect as the day i
found it, ready for its next owner
and with a smile on my face and love in my
heart, i owe nothing but thanks to ms. cruella de
vil
maybe we can all learn something from her

**- biology was never my strong suit,
it's a good thing you're smarter
than me**

you have such a hold on my heart i think there
are even traces of you in my bloodstream
fingerprints like kiss marks on my arteries
i can feel my desire for you cupped beautifully
around my aorta
but i bet if we checked your heart for dna we
would never find mine
it was stupid of me to think that i could ever
imprint myself on you like that
like i could ever leave an everlasting mark
to show i was there
to show i am here
to mark my territory
but i guess you were never my territory to mark
simply a passerby who allowed me to imagine
what it would feel like to have my heart filled
with music notes
beautiful melodies
like the sound of you breathing next to me
like the sound of that awkward laugh you do
when i tell a really bad joke but you laugh
anyway so i don't complain
the sound of your lips touching mine

the sound that you make when you're thinking
or conflicted
or like the sound of you trying really hard not to
be ticklish
then the sound of you giving into being really
ticklish

- i forgot how to read music years
ago

i have to let you go soon
i can see i am hurting you
i can see pain behind your eyes
like soft mellow notes on a
piano

pain playing heartbreak
songs behind every loving
moment
minor scales hidden
between our hands
it is hurting me to see you
hurting
but like a musician clinging to her instrument in
her final days i don't know how to put you down

- before you go, please come back

before you go
i don't know what this is but it's for you
or at least about you
a collection of poems and things i never told you
and never knew i felt
but i guess now you're gone it's time to say it
so…

before you go
as i write this
i have had a horrible day
i have got 'jealous' by labrinth on repeat
i haven't eaten dinner
on top of all that, it is the first time in months we
have gone an entire 24 hours and counting
without speaking
i can feel myself losing you
and so here we are
writing heartbreak poetry at 2am
what a cliche

before you go
i have so much to thank you for
you gave me endless mornings of waking up and
feeling like i had slumbered in poetry

a mirage of metaphors falling out of my
fingertips as soon as my eyes open
and that wasn't even on the best of days

before you go
is now the right time to tell you there are nights i
would lie awake thinking of the day i wouldn't
have to say goodbye
or goodnight
or i love you, see you later
i would go to sleep in anticipation of the day i
would say i love you, turn around and still feel
every piece of your love radiating of me like a
shooting star
i wanted to breathe in sync with you for entire
evenings as if our lungs were one and would
never break apart
but i guess i've survived for so long breathing on
my own, continuing to do so won't be so bad,
right?
at least i might actually get some sleep
i just have to stop dancing with the moon
stop replacing your hand on my cheek with
teardrops
having my eyes glaze over when i think of you
for the wrong reasons
then i might actually say goodnight, turn around
and just sleep

before you go
i think about you
all the time

we never broke up because we were never
together
but i can see us just drifting apart
to that weird hemisphere of empty space
between friends and strangers
the 'a' word
acquaintances
what we always said we will never become
but there's only so many kisses we can miss
before two becomes one and one
but
still i think you are going to be my favourite ex
i say that because even though i can see our
future reflected in the light of your eye
i'm not sure you've got the same vision
just slightly impaired
living in 2021 without 2020 vision
what does it feel like to navigate the world
without a muse
without a driving desire pushing you to be better
without a love who makes you smile
you see i would feel sorry for you
but it's okay
i don't need glasses

i can see a love beyond your imagination for the
both of us
hold my hand and i will lead you to a sight so
beautiful it's blinding
i know it's crazy to think of anything more
beautiful than you
but it's out there
i can see it so clearly
so it doesn't matter if you're going to be my
favourite ex
because right now
you're simply my favourite
and even if we never get back together
i want the next person i fall in love with to be
someone i can talk to about you
endless nights of talking about my favourite
person
what could be better?

before you go
if right now isn't for us
i hope we meet again
because when i kiss you i can taste the next fifty
years on your lips
which means i'm gonna know you in fifty years
time
so even if those fifty years don't happen exactly
as i imagine
i hope that in fifty years time

i can still stare into your eyes
and get lost in the golden specks staring back at
me
but i think i'm forgetting what your lips tasted
like
i used to be able to kiss you and taste our future
lingering in the corner of your smile
but now
i can't even remember what it felt like

before you go
what if i wait for you for the rest of my life and
you never come back?
what do i do then?
settle for the next best thing with however many
years i have left?
forever thinking of what could have been
living my life with the thought of you forever
lingering in my frontal lobe
or do i give up?
and finally realise that love wasn't meant for me
because i don't think i can do this again
and i don't think i want to

before you go
the truth is if the world ended tomorrow
if everyone descended into complete chaos and
panic at the end our universe
if we had 24 hours left to live

here's what i would do
i would order a nando's - 5 hot wings, garlic
bread and peri salted chips
i would take 5 shots of bacardi
i would probably watch one last episode of
eastenders - just for luck
i would call my mum, my brother, my friends
and i would apologise
i would apologise for the fact that i would be
choosing to spend my remaining 23 hours with
you
without a doubt

before you go
did you know i still drink your favourite tea
sipping on peppermint flavourings with our
memories infused into every droplet
i can't stop drinking it
finding myself in the supermarket
subconsciously dropping teabags that i don't
even like into my basket
but it reminds me of what your breath feels like
on the back of my neck
of all your bad habits
of everything i don't want to forget
of everything i can't let go of yet
and if i stop i fear that may be our last straw
that the handle may fall off our mug
and we'll shatter into pieces

or i will at least
who knew peppermint tea would become so
important to me
i've gone from never drinking tea in my life, to
clutching tea bags like my life depends on it
burning my tongue on hot watered impatience
because the memory of you tastes too sweet to
wait for

before you go
i think everyone has that person who teaches
them that overthinking does not make them over
love you
for me
i think you were that person
i think you overstayed your welcome
i would happily have you reside in me for the
rest of our lives but not in the way in which you
let yourself in
you turned the key a bit too aggressively with no
regard for how you left the lock once you'd
closed the door behind you
i want to feel loved without having to beg for it
i wanted a love that felt like summer
instead i got a tornado amidst a windstorm in the
wintery months
sweeping up my already crumbling foundations

and i think for the first time i can finally admit
you were a bomb in my life who never thought
of diffusing their threat themselves
only making it worse
there are times when i wouldn't want to speak to
you because i knew how it would end
i knew i would end the call and just cry
press that red button and have tears fall out of
me like music notes
but the tune wouldn't be quite so melodic
a wail of disjointed sounds in a soundcloud mix
of emotions
my heart dropping before the beat does
me forgiving him before the end of the first
verse
remembering the call
remembering how much he doesn't want me and
crying again repeatedly by the end of the bridge
holding down my live lock screen of us, with
tears chasing down my face, became the chorus
loop to every phone call
in that empty shower
on the floor
cradling myself and all my scars
having the dark seduce me just like you
i became the album cover to every breakup
playlist that should never have been written
that made 'euphoria' feel like 'teletubbies'

that made me less alone in something i had no
intention of ever feeling

before you go
i once heard
that you know you're in love when the space
between a person's ear and eye
feels like home
maybe that's why when i hug you i can smell a
white picket fence and four kids calling our
names
i used to think you could hear it too
i hope one day you will
even if it's not with me

before you go
we have an entire summer of frolicking in
sunsets and chasing down dreams ahead of us
before we are catapulted into entirely different
universes
until you are sharing your love, your smiles,
yourself with someone else
so, my love,
i know we have said goodbye a thousand times
before and even if we truly meant it last time
please know
if there was even the slightest chance that we
both hid our lie behind the widest of smiles
i will take you back in a heartbeat

the same way that very heartbeat will belong to
you for the rest of our lives
i think we just take star crossed lovers a bit too
literally

before you go
there's one more thing i never told you
but i know it wouldn't have made you stay if i
did and i know you will never hear this
mi amor
mi marido
and everything else we used to call each other
here it is
te quiero
te quiero mucho
i love you so much

before you go...
can you hold me again?
let me see you one last time
and we can create a forever out of numerous one
last times
so i can engrave you in my memory
just to make sure i never forget a single element
of your face
...before you come back

- i promise i'm not a jealous person... ish

5 things you shouldn't be jealous of when you
weren't even dating

your spotify (i really can't
explain this one)
the tv you watch without me
your favourite pillow
it will always be my favourite
too, even if it never belonged
to me either
your cups of tea
because you're sipping on them instead of me
the books you don't read because no matter how
much you ignore them you still keep them
around
i wish i could be an unread book of yours for the
rest of my life

the biggest thing i shouldn't be jealous of is the
fact that you're not jealous of my tears
you're not jealous that every night there is
something else caressing my cheeks
another thing keeping me awake at night
another thing replacing your fingers on my lips

another reason as to why my eyes glaze over
when i think of you
you don't even think of that
i'm jealous because i would trade anything to
touch your cheeks one more time

- i hope i never lose my memory

the memories these walls keep, i wish they could
speak
so i could relive you touching me
so i could relive all the conversations i've had
without you there
where i've told you everything i'm too scared to
tell you
where i tell you everything i want to tell you
and those times when you were just a phone call
away
my walls hold memories you may never learn of
but i want them to hold memories of which you
are present

memories of which you are right there
touching my walls
imprinting fingertips onto them
engraving new memories with your name onto
them
showing my walls that they don't always need to
maintain such pain underneath their plaster
they can be happy

they can hold memories of me being held
of me being loved

of your nose touching mine as my hands trace
the blemishes of your cheeks
i think you will be the one to show my walls
what i look like when i'm truly happy

- tangled is the best disney film. no debate necessary.

i want to fall in love in with someone who says
they love me most when i say i love them more
i want to fall in love with my flynn rider
but maybe a 'mother gothel' love is all i'm
destined for?

- i have tasted immortality

when do we stop calling this young love?
when do we stop undermining the possible
eternity of our feelings?
when do we stop fighting shared breaths in the
name of immaturity?

because the future is no longer far away
we do not have the same time to find other fish
in the sea as we did when we were bouncing in
our youthful sunrises
the sun has already set on our childhood
and we are swimming towards new challenges
that children do not face
this is not young love anymore

this is not a kiss on the cheek easily forgotten for
the other pair of eyes staring at me across the
playground
this is an overwhelming sense of admiration for
the only one who was able to take me and my
childhood and let me grow wings big enough to
fly away from it
this is just love

and without you
i have never known sadness like this before

and i truly believe that i was made to always be
a little bit sad
like all my happy moments will forever be
tinged in droplets of melancholy
but this is a different level
this is not the same sadness i felt in the nurses'
office after a graze on my childhood knees
this is as if my entire soul has fallen into a vat of
sorrow
my soul feels like harley quinn
falling into her demise
further and further from her lover
to the point where she is no longer recognisable
to herself
to anyone
to her 10-year-old self who thought the world
was her oyster and that there were plenty of
other fish in the sea

i guess as a child you never truly believe people
will just pack up and leave when they promised
to never do so
i know this is not young love because i no longer
have faith in a pinky promise
but then again maybe it is
because you made me feel like i was on top of
the world
i would find myself walking around wearing the
smile you gave me

you took my father's responsibility
held my heart on your shoulders
allowed me to look over the crowd
over the trauma of past lives lived
over the friends lost
over the pain
to a future that held only us
to the bus route that i have memorised like the
back of my hand because it took me to you
to the bridge that we fell in love on that i see on
my journey every day
to the memories that float across my eyes as i
close them and fall asleep
to the songs i used to sing to you
to the lines of poetry you fell asleep to
to the tears of joy i cried simply because you
hugged me

but it's times like these
when i'm walking down the street
when i have passed my old school and the bridge
we fell in love on in the same journey
when i'm wearing your hat
with your chain around my neck
wearing the trousers i know you like
texting you on the way to my next stop
when i simply can't believe you could ever hurt
me so effortlessly
so consistently

so softly
it's times like these when i wish the mind would
shed its memories so i can fall in love with you
all over again
but do it right this time
i can barely remember my childhood so those
memories are expendable to me if that means i
could get a second chance to prove that this
that us
that we
are meant to last past adolescence
so i can walk down the street
passing my old school and the bridge we fell in
love on in the same journey
wearing your hat
with your chain around my neck
wearing the trousers i know you like
but
with your hand in mine too

because this life we lead is too short
two decades of our lives have almost flashed
past
and we will all die
unless you become the next person to
immortalise humanity
we will die
and yes

sometimes he makes me feel like everyday i am
dying
but
even if six days a week i am knocking on death's
door
conversing with the grim reaper
face to face with a black hole of despair
there is one day a week to look forward to
one day of unadulterated bliss
and i will spend the rest of my life, in the
eventuality that you don't end up immortalising
humanity, trying to make that one day my
everyday

because when i feel his cheek against mine
i know that is a feeling i will choose above
everything else
i will not teeter that feeling on the edge
exchanging it for a maybe
maybe i will find someone else
maybe someone else will love me
maybe someone will cherish the very same
things in me that i cherish in him
but they are not him
he is not a maybe to me
so
if the end of the world comes

and by some likely stroke of luck you haven't
managed to stop the ticking clock of life from
getting arthritis
i will be okay
i will come and sit with you
commend you for your efforts
listen to you as you reminisce on young love
hold your hand as you drift off to sleep
because loving him makes me feel immortal
already
and if i have tasted immortality on his lips
this could never be just…
young love

- the dream that made me a tea drinker

"what makes you happy?" he asked
to which i responded "reading poetry that feels
like a warm of cup of tea"
we stared at each other
i noticed the corner of his lips turn up in laughter
and i knew exactly what he was going to say

…

"but you don't drink tea"
we both burst into laughter at yet another one of
my metaphors that made no sense
but isn't that what a good poem is all about?

- 'i fell in love with him the way you fall asleep, slowly, and then all at once' - the fault in our stars

i still remember the moment i fell in love with
you
our first trip to london
late coming home, as i always am with you
you were laughing at how i'd said your favourite
phrase earlier
and i swear i fell in love with you in that split
second
you looked beautiful
eyes crinkled, smile wide, dimples on show,
playing with your fingers
the harsh train light bounced off your skin and
the other passengers simply fell away with it

they weren't invited into our world, you see
we were on our own island
the beauty of your smile felt like my little secret
that no one else knew of
your eyes glazed over just enough for those
same golden specks to appear
for my heartbeat to be visible in the reflection
you looked majestic

like the physical epitome of what i imagine
heaven to be
and i couldn't help but smile too

watching you carefully from the seat across from
you
trying to imprint every crevice into my mind in
the hope that i'd never forget this moment
this beauty
this love
and after this poem
i don't think i ever will

- x makes the world go round for me

your face reminds me of poetry
there are beautiful metaphors hidden in your
eyes
melodic rhythms wrapped inside the curls of
your hair
perfectly placed stanzas intertwined within your
footsteps
i can feel the joy of a finished poem inside your
smile
but you're a mathematician so let me put you
into a formula you'd prefer
you = poetry, but poetry = x
now, read the title again

- loves of my life

i would lay down my life for you
it's true
i would lay down my life for you, because if it
wasn't for you my life would have been laid
down already

i would give you my everything
my soul
my love
my time
i'd lend you everything i own
the parts of me that are not even ready to be
given
in exchange for your smile
i'd hold your happiness within my fingertips like
the very oxygen i need to breathe
like i possess the very elements needed to make
the universe go round

i would rather fall to my death than see a flicker
of pain in your eyes
i would rather close my eyes to all the world has
to offer than to be able to give you anything but
the joy you deserve
i would rather die than see a frown on your face

because you are family i chose and will keep on
choosing until the day that i die

my loves deserve the world
they deserve to be bolstered into the universe
around the stars where they belong
to sit amongst galaxies
being able to pick and choose which universes to
enter
because their futures are as bright as shooting
stars
blinding with possibility
sparkling with talent
guiding them towards a future with the utmost
promise

i have spent so many years alone with no
shooting stars
navigating through the darkness by myself
i have had romantic affairs with loneliness
but amidst all the madness this past year has had
to offer
it has also provided me with a plate of gold
a plate of something to be treasured
a plate with all of you
a plate of light
light that can finally lead towards the right path
a path well travelled
a path imprinted by somebody else's footprints

not just my own anymore
a path that is more than needed

i simply feel like the luckiest girl in the world
and i can't wait to teach my kids about love

but you, you, have the power to break my heart
more than anyone i know

because there are times when i think that you
couldn't hate me more than anyone in the world
it may be all in my head but
it is all i can think about
and in those moments
when i want to run and hide from all love has to
offer
you are there
with a text, with a call, with a hug
with something to give my star its own gravity
back
just something to remind me that you are the
reason i feel so alive

there's so much i didn't know i didn't know
until i met you
until i met you, until i met you, until i met you
there's so much i didn't know i didn't know
because you all taught me something i didn't
know i didn't know

i didn't know i was worthy of your love
i'm still unsure of that
but i will forever pour my love down your
throats until you're choking on every ounce of
happiness i wish for you to endure
because you are more than worthy of mine

you make me spell love "N A K E D"
loving you has been a choice to live naked and i
think i am okay with that
because your love is a doctor that can cure all
my ailments but still asks where the wounds
come from
your love is what i need to pry me into the future
even though the past still has its claws in me
your love makes me want to give up every secret
part of me and leave no secret untold
your love is the thing i need to live but
everything i am willing to die for

my biggest fear would be to see you die
me and the grim reaper have a checkered past
but to have you plucked from the centre of my
universe
to have my planets navigating around your loss
it's something my heart couldn't take
it's something that would make my heart break
it is my BIGGEST fear

and i hope, with every fibre of my being, i hope
that it never comes true

the day our love drifts off in the wind
as we go our separate ways
as time dismantles our universe and our galaxy
of stars float away
my heart will break
into a thousand tiny pieces
but those pieces will be sprinkled with happiness
like fairy dust
floating to the sky
because, i know, wherever you may be
even if we never speak again for the rest of our
lives
even if you are across galaxies giving your
smiles to someone else
i know
i will always, always, lay down my life for you.

**- he started writing poetry after
meeting me**

"felt like home so i called her febreeze."